HOW TO DRAW MONSTERS

HOW TO DRAW KING KONG

Derrick Richards

Enslow PUBLISHING

Please visit our website, www.enslow.com. For a free color catalog of all our high-quality books,
call toll free 1-800-398-2504 or fax 1-877-980-4454

Published in 2027 by
Enslow Publishing
2544 Clinton Street
Buffalo, NY 14224

Portions of this work were originally authored by Greg Roza and published as *Drawing Movie Monsters Step-by-Step: Drawing King Kong.* All new material in this edition is authored by Derrick Richards.

Cataloging-in-Publication Data
Names: Richards, Derrick.
Title: How to draw King Kong / Derrick Richards.
Description: Buffalo, NY : Enslow Publishing, 2027. | Series: How to draw monsters | Includes glossary and index.
Identifiers: ISBN 9781978548695 (pbk.) | ISBN 9781978548701 (library bound) | ISBN 9781978548718 (ebook)
Subjects: LCSH: Monsters in art--Juvenile literature. | Drawing--Technique--Juvenile literature. | King Kong (Fictitious character) in art.
Classification: LCC NC825.M6 R534 2027 | DDC 743.87--dc23

Printed in China

Photos Credits: Cover, p. 1 WIRACHAIPHOTO/Shutterstock.com; cover, p. 1 Wisnu Gareng; cover, p. 1, 5, 7, 9, 11, 13, 15, 17, 19, 21 (notebook) Liena10/Shutterstock.com; p. 5 (ruler) karen roach/Shutterstock.com; p. 5 (colored pencils) Avocado_studio/Shutterstock.com; p. 5 (marker) New Africa/Shutterstock.com; p. 6 hbll-scmwiki/Wikipedia; p. 8, 10, 12, 14, 18, Wikipedia/Wikipedia; p. 16 pngtree.com; p. 20 Sharkshock/Shutterstock.com; p. 22 Shutterstock AI/Shutterstock.com

CPSIA compliance information: Batch #QSENS27: For further information, contact Enslow Publishing, New York, New York, at 1-800-398-2504.

CONTENTS

IT'S KING KONG!

On a faraway island, the ground rumbles beneath your feet. Giant footsteps sound like thunder. What's that emerging through the thick trees? It's King Kong!

Since his first movie in 1933, this movie monster has been scaring fans of all ages. King Kong looks like a ferocious gorilla that stands more than 50 feet (15 m) tall! He can pick up a person and carry them in the palm of his hand. People have been fascinated by this fearsome beast for nearly 100 years. Let's learn to draw this classic movie monster in a few easy steps!

You will need the following supplies:

PAPER

RULER

PENCIL

MARKER

COLORED PENCILS

KING OF THE JUNGLE

King Kong is a classic movie monster that was **inspired** by "lost world" stories of the early 1900s. These were stories about the discovery of places that seemed like they were from a time long ago. Writers like Arthur Conan Doyle and Edgar Rice Burroughs made these stories very popular.

Many of the lost world stories included ancient animals, such as dinosaurs. These giant animals inspired Merian C. Cooper to create a giant gorilla named King Kong.

First, let's try drawing King Kong as he prepares to attack.

King Kong's creator was a pilot during World War I. Cooper searched the world for **adventure**. He also liked writing and making movies.

Step 1

Draw an oval for the face. Add the outline of the body.

Step 2

Draw eight ovals to guide you in drawing the arms and legs. Add lines to form the shoulders.

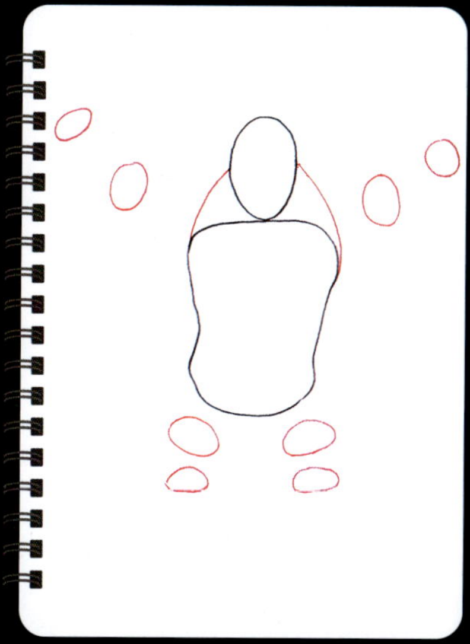

Step 3

Join the ovals with lines to form the arms and legs. Add the outlines of the hands and feet.

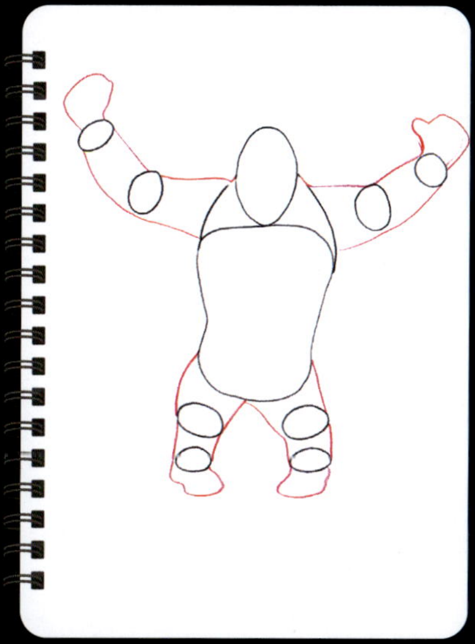

Step 4

Draw the fingers and the toes. Add a rectangular shape to the chest. Erase extra lines.

Step 5

Add the outlines of the facial features. Draw the claws and the fur. Erase the guides.

Step 6

Add details to the facial features. Add more fur. Erase extra lines. Now color your drawing.

A STAR IN THE MAKING

King Kong made his movie **debut** in 1933. In the movie *King Kong*, the young actress Ann Darrow is looking for adventure. She joins a film crew that is going to the **exotic** Skull Island.

Things take a bad turn as Ann is **kidnapped** by natives of Skull Island. They tie her up and give her to King Kong. But—surprise!—the giant gorilla falls in love with her. He protects her as soldiers try to get her back.

King Kong often battles people but also takes on other movie monsters. Let's try drawing King Kong as he battles a dinosaur!

Ann Darrow was played by Canadian actress Fay Wray. She earned the role partly because she was a good screamer!

Step 1

Draw an oval for each creature's head. Add the outlines of their bodies.

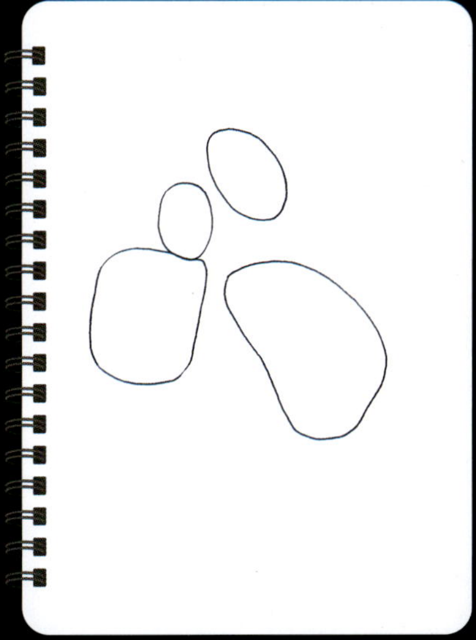

Step 2

Add guide shapes as shown. Add lines to join the heads to the bodies.

Step 3

Join the guide shapes using lines to form the arms, legs, and tail.

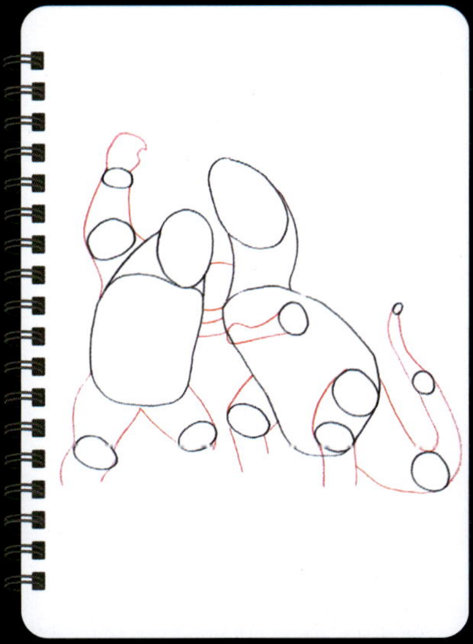

Step 4

Draw the outlines of the faces and the hands. Add a shape for King Kong's chest. Draw the stick in King Kong's hand. Add the outline of the grass and bushes.

Step 5

Add the facial features, claws, and fur. Add details to the bushes. Erase the guide shapes.

Step 6

Add details to the faces and the rest of the scene. Draw scales, teeth, and fur. Erase extra lines.

KONG IN NEW YORK

The story of the 1933 film continues with the filmmakers rescuing Ann and capturing King Kong. They take the monster from Skull Island to New York City. But King Kong escapes and kidnaps Ann again! In a classic scene, King Kong climbs to the top of the Empire State Building with her. Airplanes attack the monster but Kong fights back. Finally, the giant gorilla falls to his death. But don't worry, Ann makes it down safely!

Now, let's try drawing King Kong as he climbs up the side of the building.

The movie was such a success that its **sequel**, *Son of Kong*, was released later that same year.

Step 1
Draw two round shapes for the head and the body.

Step 2
Add smaller circles and ovals to use as guides for the arms and legs.

Step 3
Use the guide shapes to draw the arms and legs. Begin the hands and feet. Add a line for the building.

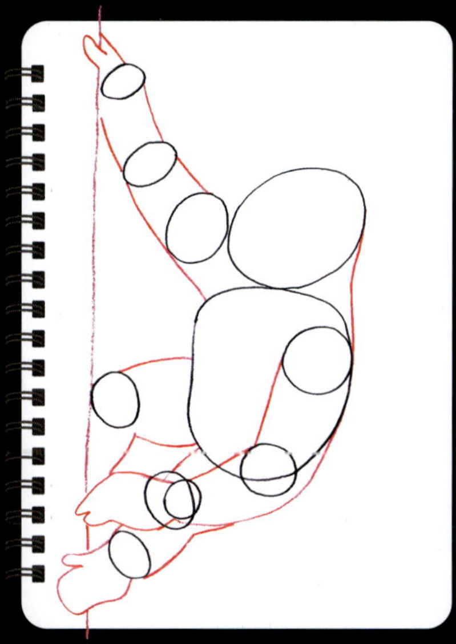

Step 4
Draw the outline of the chest. Add the outlines of the face, leg, fingers, and toes.

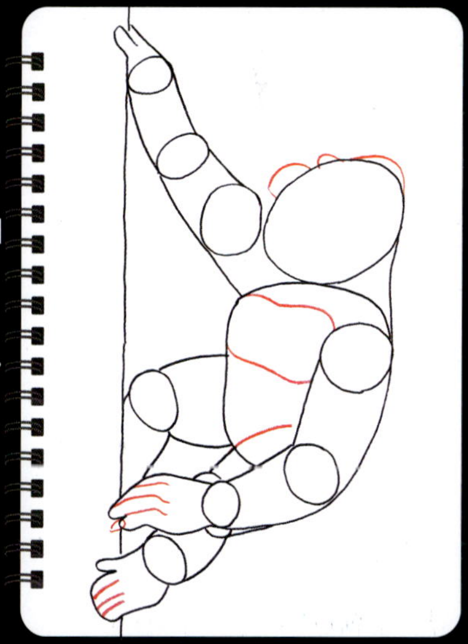

Step 5
Draw the claws and the facial features. Add some fur. Add details to the building. Erase the guide shapes.

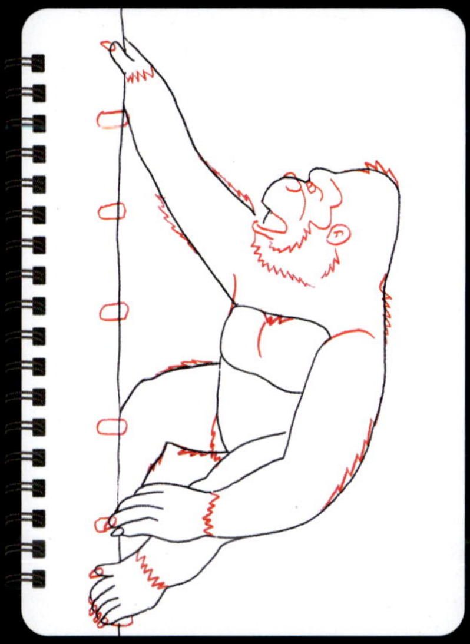

Step 6
Finish your drawing by adding details to the facial features, the building, and the fur. Erase extra lines.

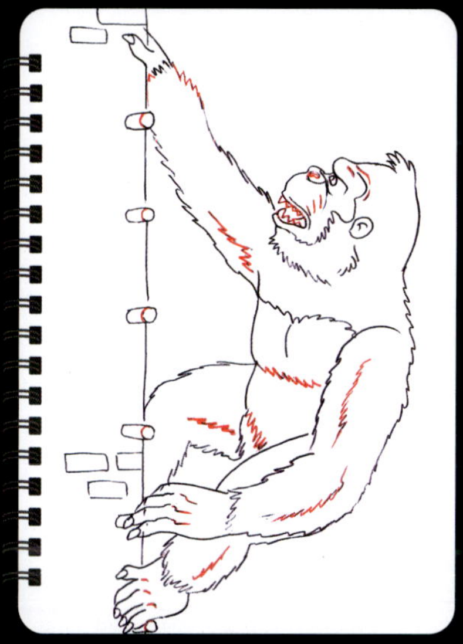

KONG COMES TO LIFE

King Kong was a giant ape. He towered above trees and buildings. How did filmmakers make him look so big? The people who made *King Kong* in 1933 used a **special effect** called stop-motion photography. First, a photographer takes a picture of a model of a gorilla. Next, the model is moved very slightly, and another picture is taken.

The photographer repeats this process over and over again. The pictures are shown one after another so the gorilla looks like it is moving by itself!

Now, let's draw this huge beast as he towers over buildings and carries Ann in the palm of his hand.

No one knows exactly how tall King Kong is. His height keeps changing, even throughout the same movie!

Step 1

Draw an oval for the head. Add the outline of the body.

Step 2

Draw guide shapes around the body.

Step 3

Draw lines to join the guides and form the arms and legs. Begin to draw the hands.

Step 4

Add fingers to the hands. Draw a woman in King Kong's left hand. Draw the buildings.

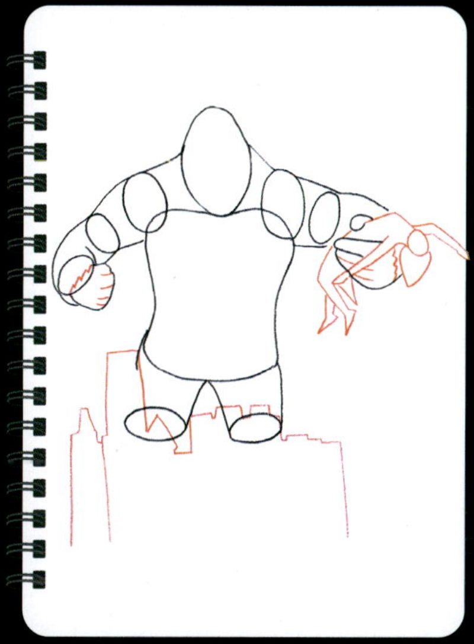

Step 5

Add fur, claws, and other details to King Kong and Ann. Add lines to the buildings. Erase the guide shapes.

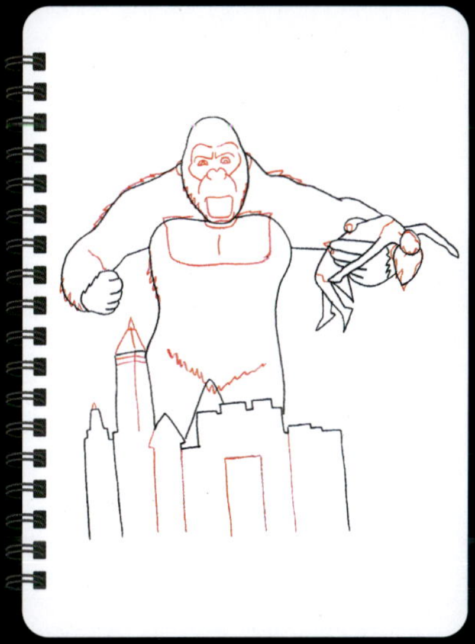

Step 6

Add the final details to King Kong and Ann. Add windows and other details to the buildings. Erase extra lines.

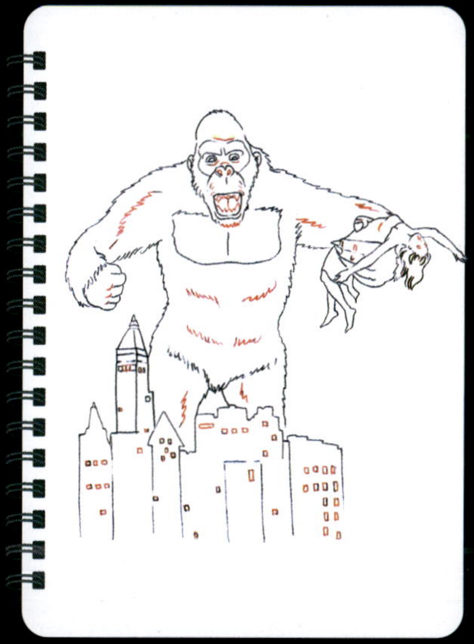

A MONSTER-MOVIE STAR

The 1933 **version** of *King Kong* was a huge success. It was a very scary movie for its time, and **horror** movie fans loved to be scared! At the same time, audiences also loved cheering for the giant beast.

In the 1930s, *King Kong* did not win any movie awards. Since that time, however, it has won many awards for its special effects and its importance as a film. Even today it is considered one of the best movies ever made.

Let's draw King Kong as he stands atop the Empire State Building and swats planes out of the sky.

King Kong is often shown as both a terrifying monster and a lovable hero.

Step 1

Draw an oval for the head. Add a larger shape for the outline of the body.

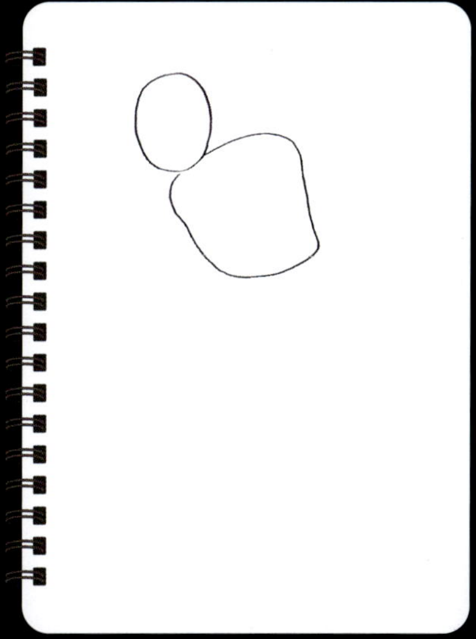

Step 2

Add ovals around the body as shown. Connect the head to the body with a curved line.

Step 3

Draw lines to connect the ovals to form the arms and legs. Add the outlines of the hands and the feet.

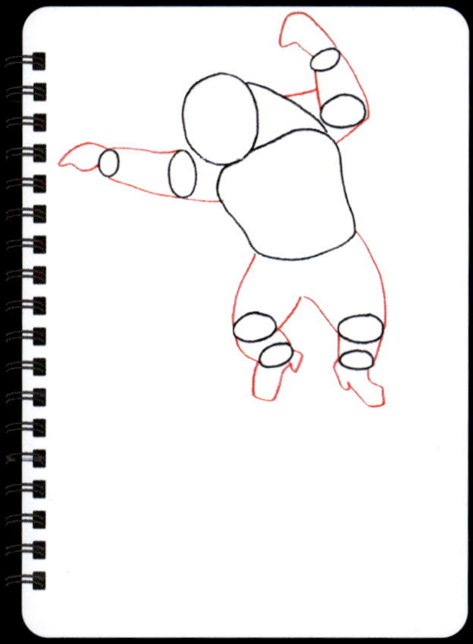

Step 4

Add a curved line to the top of the head. Add lines for the fingers and toes. Draw the outlines of the airplanes and the building.

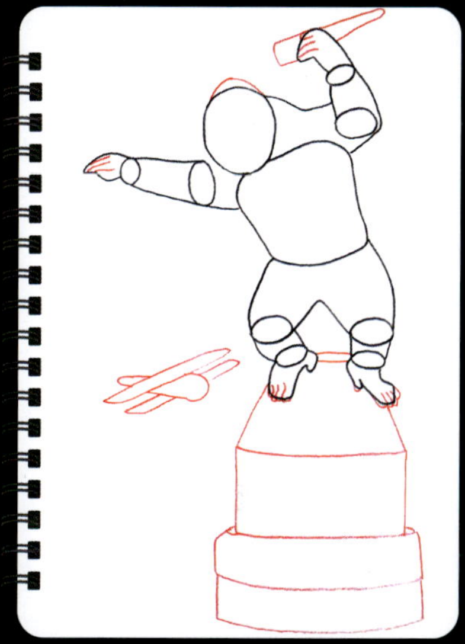

Step 5

Begin to add facial features, claws, and fur. Add details to the airplanes and the building. Erase the guide shapes.

Step 6

Finish your drawing by adding more details to the face, fur, airplanes, and building. Erase extra lines. Finish your drawing by adding color.

KING KONG CONTINUES

Since the 1930s, filmmakers have made many more movies about King Kong. In *Son of Kong*, a man from the first movie returns to Skull Island in search of treasure. He meets Kong's son, who is much smaller. Kong's son saves the main characters from a giant bear!

In 1962, King Kong battled another famous movie monster in *King Kong vs. Godzilla*. American filmmakers remade *King Kong* in 1976. Jessica Lange played the part that Fay Wray played in the 1933 film.

Now, let's draw King Kong in the moment before he breaks out of those chains!

The 1976 film won an Academy Award for Best Visual Effects.

Step 1

Draw an oval for the head. Add a large shape for the outline of the body.

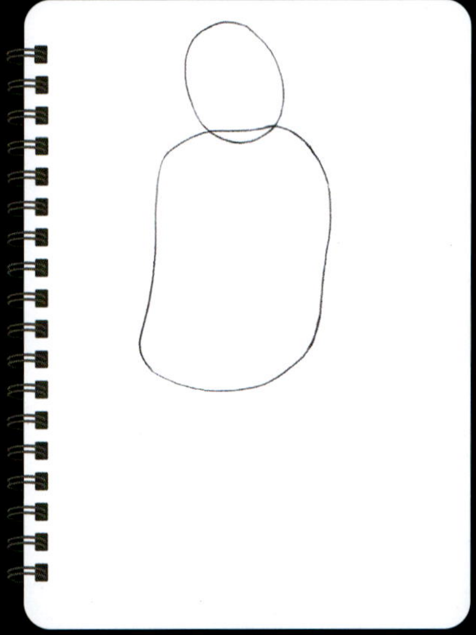

Step 2

Add small round shapes around the body.

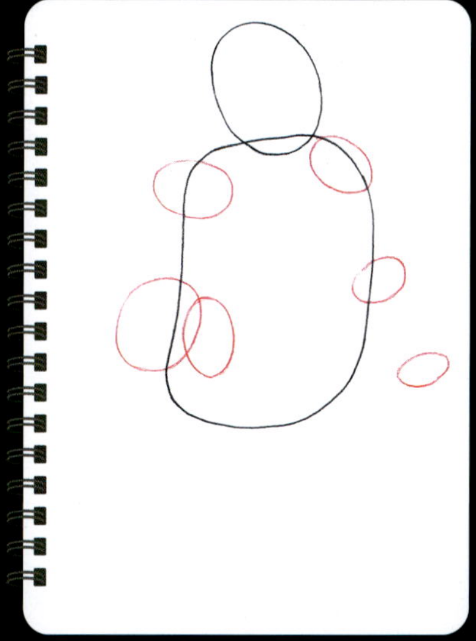

Step 3

Draw curved lines to form the shoulders, arms, and lower body.

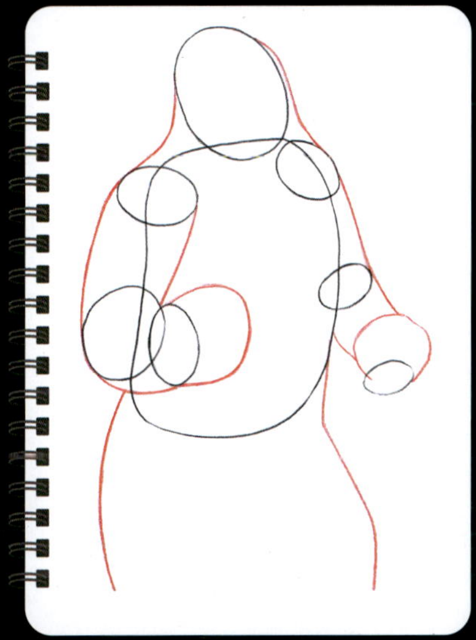

Step 4

Add fur to the face and body. Draw the fingers and an ear. Add the chains that hold King Kong's wrists.

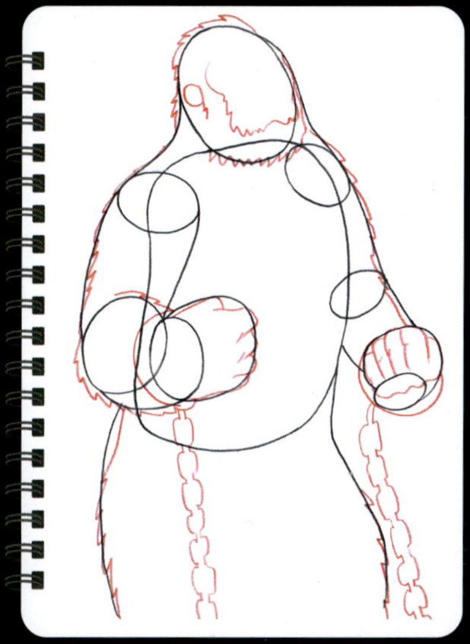

Step 5

Draw the facial features and the outline of the chest. Add more fur. Finish drawing the chains. Erase round guides.

Step 6

Add the teeth. Finish the facial features and the fur. Erase extra lines.

A MODERN-DAY KONG

Ann and Kong meet again in the 2005 remake, *King Kong*. It tells the same story as the 1933 movie and is even set during the same time period. However, this time filmmakers used computers to create a more realistic-looking King Kong. This made the giant monster scarier than ever before!

The new King Kong was also smarter. He used **sign language** to talk to Ann. This time, Ann was played by British actress Naomi Watts. Let's draw King Kong as he roams the streets of New York City.

King Kong repeats the sign for "beautiful" when communicating with Ann. Other movies show him communicating in different ways.

Step 1

Draw an oval for the head. Add the outline of the body.

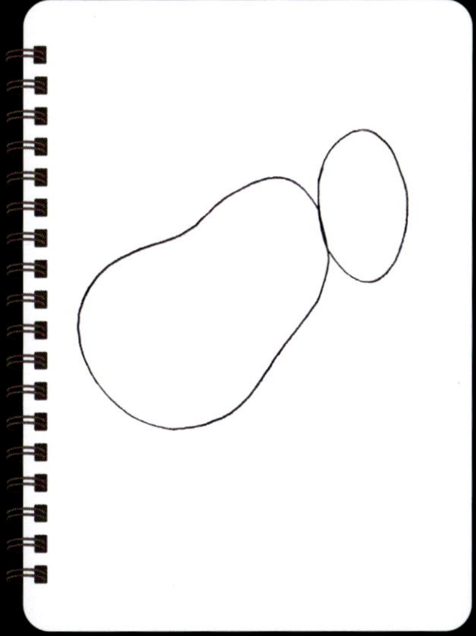

Step 2

Draw round shapes around the body. These will guide you in drawing the arms and legs.

Step 3

Join the guide shapes to form the arms and legs. Add lines for the neck, hands, and feet.

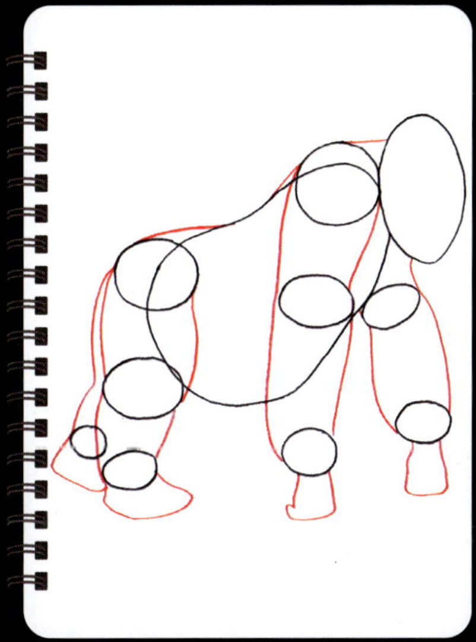

Step 4

Add details to the hands and feet. Erase extra lines.

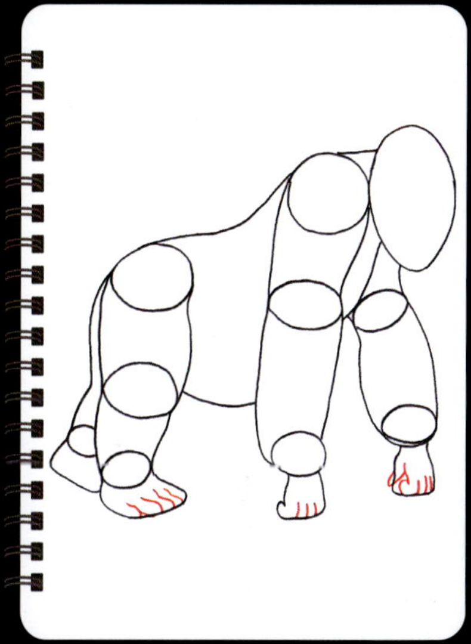

Step 5

Draw the facial features. Add the claws and the fur. Erase the guide shapes.

Step 6

Add details to the face and the fur. Erase extra lines.

KING OF THE BEASTS

King Kong is still as popular as ever. He has most recently returned to the big screen in 2021's *Godzilla vs. Kong* and 2024's *Godzilla x Kong: The New Empire*. In these two movies, King Kong clashes with one of his biggest rivals, monster-movie star Godzilla. Godzilla is a giant dinosaur that first appeared in a Japanese movie in the 1950s, and since then has become an international **icon**.

Finally, let's draw King Kong as he beats his chest and lets out a mighty roar. This monster is truly the king of the beasts!

The giant gorilla is more than a movie star. His likeness has been featured in books, cartoons, comics, video games, and television shows.

Step 1

Draw an oval for the head. Draw the outline of the body below the oval.

Step 2

Add round guide shapes as shown.

Step 3

Join the round shapes to form the arms and legs. Add the outlines of the hands and feet.

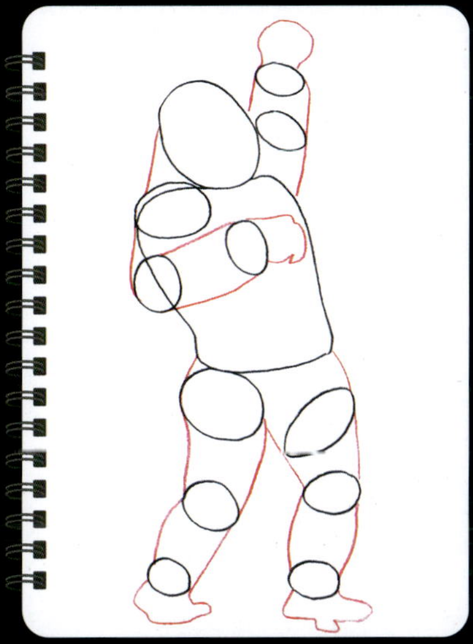

Step 4

Draw King Kong's fingers and toes.

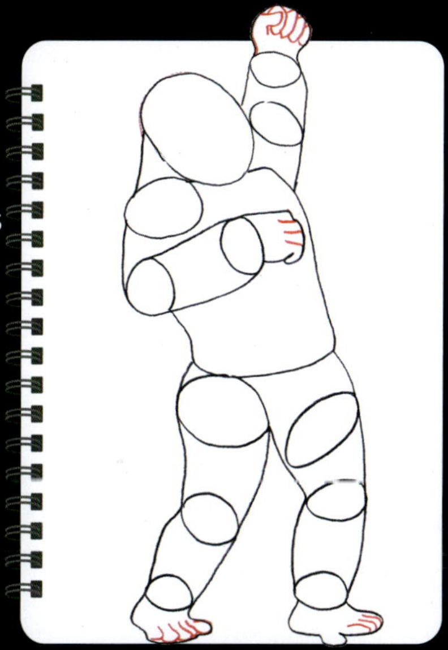

Step 5

Add lines to the chest. Draw the facial features. Give King Kong claws and fur. Erase the guides.

Step 6

Add details to the facial features and the fur. Draw the ground. Erase extra lines. Color your drawing.

DID YOU KNOW?

Several scenes were taken out of the original 1933 *King Kong* because they were believed to be too scary. One scene featured a giant man-eating spider!

For the 1933 movie, filmmakers created a giant King Kong head and two giant King Kong hands. They were used for close-up shots.

King Kong's fierce roar was created by playing a lion's and tiger's growl at the same time, then playing them backward.

The 2005 remake of *King Kong* cost $207 million to make. At the time, this was the most money ever spent on a movie!

Filmmakers spent $500,000 to make *King Kong* in 1933. Most movies at the time cost much less.

Since 1933, King Kong has starred in more than a dozen movies.

GLOSSARY

adventure (ed-VEN-chur) An unusual or exciting thing to do.

debut (day-BYOO) A first appearance or performance.

exotic (ig-ZAH-tik) From a faraway country.

horror (HOR-ur) Something that makes people feel shock or fear.

icon (EYE-kahn) Something that is widely admired for having influence.

inspired (in-SPYRD) To have moved someone to do something.

kidnap (KID-nap) To take a person away by force.

sequel (SEE-kwuhl) A book or movie that continues the story of an earlier work.

sign language (SYN LANG-wij) A language in which hand motions stand for words or ideas.

special effects (SPEH-shul uh-FEKTS) Tricks in moviemaking that make scenes that are fake look real.

version (VER-zhun) A thing that is different from something else, or that has different forms.

INDEX

ON THE INTERNET

King Kong Facts for Kids

https://kids.kiddle.co/King_Kong

Learn more about the history of this classic movie monster.

How to Watch Every King Kong Movie in Order

https://movieweb.com/king-kong-movies-in-order/

See a list of all the King Kong films and read more about them.